EGYPTIAN MYTHOLOGY

OSIRIS

BY SAMANTHA S. BELL

CONTENT CONSULTANT
KASIA SZPAKOWSKA, PhD
PROFESSOR EMERITUS OF EGYPTOLOGY

Kids Core
An Imprint of Abdo Publishing
abdobooks.com

abdobooks.com

Published by Abdo Publishing, a division of ABDO, PO Box 398166, Minneapolis, Minnesota 55439. Copyright © 2023 by Abdo Consulting Group, Inc. International copyrights reserved in all countries. No part of this book may be reproduced in any form without written permission from the publisher. Kids Core™ is a trademark and logo of Abdo Publishing.

Printed in the United States of America, North Mankato, Minnesota.
052022
092022

Cover Photos: Shutterstock Images, background; Olga Chernyak/Shutterstock Images, Osiris
Interior Photos: Malysh Falko/Shutterstock Images, 4–5, 29 (top); Shutterstock Images, 6, 10, 28 (bottom); Peter Hermes Furian/Shutterstock Images, 9; Bas Photo/Shutterstock Images, 12; Joe and Clair Carnegie/Moment Open/Getty Images, 14–15; Espixx/Alamy, 16, 28 (top); World History Archive/Alamy, 19; Ivy Close Images/Alamy, 20, 24, 29 (bottom); iStockphoto, 22–23; Album/Alamy, 26

Editor: Layna Darling
Series Designer: Ryan Gale

Library of Congress Control Number: 2021952321

Publisher's Cataloging-in-Publication Data

Names: Bell, Samantha S., author.
Title: Osiris / by Samantha S. Bell
Description: Minneapolis, Minnesota : Abdo Publishing, 2023 | Series: Egyptian mythology | Includes online resources and index.
Identifiers: ISBN 9781532198700 (lib. bdg.) | ISBN 9781644947784 (pbk.) | ISBN 9781098272357 (ebook)
Subjects: LCSH: Osiris (Egyptian deity)--Juvenile literature. | Egypt--Religion--Juvenile literature. | Gods, Egyptian--Juvenile literature. | Mythology, Egyptian--Juvenile literature.
Classification: DDC 932.01--dc23

CONTENTS

CHAPTER 1
Back from the Dead 4

CHAPTER 2
King of Egypt 14

CHAPTER 3
Osiris in Art 22

Legendary Facts 28
Glossary 30
Online Resources 31
Learn More 31
Index 32
About the Author 32

Osiris, *left*, was married to Isis, *right*. They ruled over ancient Egypt together.

BACK FROM THE DEAD

Osiris was the first king of the Egyptians. He married the goddess Isis. But his brother Seth was very jealous of him.

Seth wanted to be king, so he came up with a plan to kill Osiris. Seth made a beautiful box. He measured it to fit Osiris exactly.

Seth was Osiris's brother. He wanted to take the throne for himself.

Then Seth threw a party. He told the guests that whoever fit in the box could keep it as a gift. When Osiris climbed inside, Seth slammed down the lid and **fastened** it. The box had become a coffin. Seth threw the coffin into the Nile River. It was carried out to sea. Osiris died in the coffin.

Isis searched until she found Osiris's body. She wanted to bring him back to life. She hid Osiris in the **marshes** of the Nile River until she was ready.

A Palace Pillar

Osiris's coffin floated to the kingdom of Byblos. It became stuck in a tree on the shore. The tree grew around the coffin. The king of Byblos saw the tree. He cut it down to make a decorative pillar for his palace. Isis found the pillar and cut Osiris free.

But Seth found where Isis had hidden Osiris. To make sure Osiris stayed dead, Seth divided up his brother's body. He scattered the pieces across the land and into the Nile River. Seth was now lord of Upper Egypt.

With her sister Nephthys's help, Isis gathered the pieces. She put them together again with linen wrappings. The god of **mummification**, Anubis, helped her. Then Isis breathed life back into Osiris.

Isis became pregnant with their son, Horus. But Osiris could not stay with them. He was not fully alive or dead. He went into the **afterlife**. He became the ruler of the dead.

Osiris's coffin floated along the Nile River and into the Mediterranean Sea. The sea carried the coffin to Byblos, a kingdom on the Mediterranean Sea.

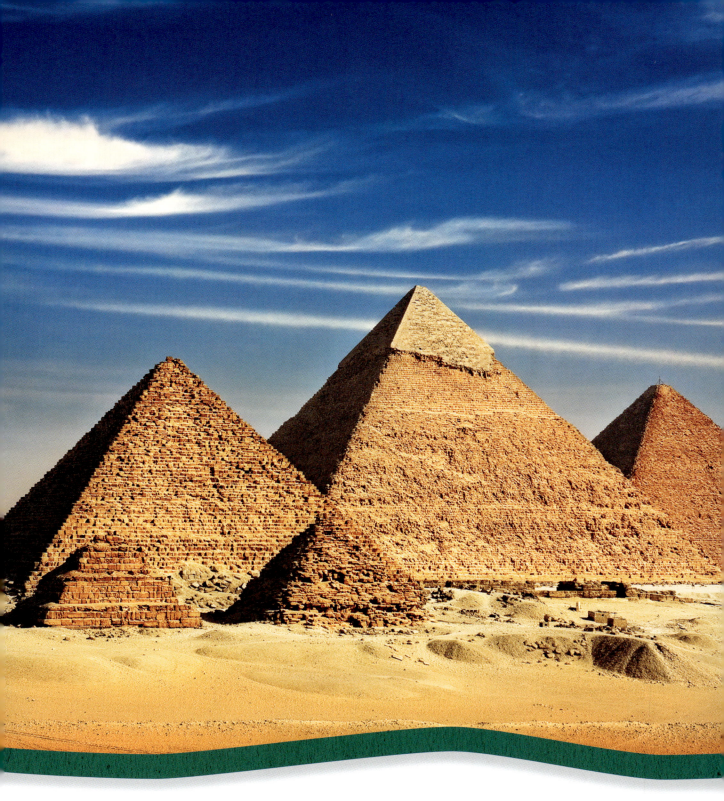

The ancient Egyptian civilization lasted for thousands of years.

Stories to Remember

Ancient Egypt was a civilization that began about 5,000 years ago. A civilization is a complex, organized society. The ancient Egyptians told many stories about their gods and goddesses. Today, these stories are called myths. Ancient Egyptians used these stories to explain why things happened the way they did. Myths explained events in nature or in everyday life. These stories talked about how the ancient Egyptian civilization began. Osiris was an important part of Egyptian mythology. Myths about Osiris helped explain what happened to people after they died.

Some myths about Osiris, *left*, were carved or painted on temple walls. This carving is at the Temple of Osiris in Abydos, Egypt.

Some myths were passed down **orally**. Others were written down in the Egyptian writing called hieroglyphs. This form of writing used pictures to describe sounds instead of letters. The myths were written on sheets of papyrus, a type of paper made from a water plant. They were also written on the walls of temples and pyramids.

PRIMARY SOURCE

Norwegian writer and teacher Jörgen Smit wrote a play about Osiris. In it, when Seth asks Osiris to try the coffin, Osiris says:

> I do not know the measurements of the coffin. Nor do I have the desire for the coffin's treasures. But I will try if it can please my brother.

Source: Jörgen Smit. "Osiris and Isis." *Waldorf Library*, n.d., waldorflibrary.org. Accessed 17 Dec. 2021.

Comparing Texts

Think about what Osiris said. Does it support the information in this chapter? Or does it give a different perspective? Explain your opinion in a few sentences.

Osiris, *left*, was one of the most well-known Egyptian gods.

KING OF EGYPT

Osiris's parents were the Earth god Geb and the sky goddess Nut. They married and had four children. The oldest was Osiris. As the oldest, he became the king of Egypt. This angered his younger brother, Seth.

The people of Osiris's kingdom loved and respected him.

Osiris became known as the god of land **fertility**. He fertilized the soil to grow large harvests. Osiris ruled as a good and wise king. The people loved and respected him. Then his brother Seth became jealous and killed him.

Before Osiris died, he had a son named Anubis. Anubis was the god of the dead and had the head of a **jackal**. He guided souls to Osiris's afterlife. After Isis brought Osiris back to life, he had a second son, Horus. He is often shown with a falcon head. After Horus grew up, he defeated Seth and became the next king of Egypt.

A Life-Giving River

The ancient Egyptians associated Osiris with the Nile River. Every year, the Nile overflows its banks. The land becomes flooded. When the water goes back down, rich soil is left behind. This makes the land good for growing crops, or fertile. To the ancient Egyptians, this **symbolized** Osiris's death and rebirth.

God of the Afterlife

Osiris became the god and chief judge of the afterlife. He decided if the souls could live with him in the Field of Reeds. This was the beautiful paradise where Osiris ruled. To get there, the souls had to go on a difficult and dangerous journey through the afterlife. They had to get past strange creatures and pass through gates and caves. They used spells to make it through.

At the end of the journey was the Hall of Judgement. In this hall, souls faced 42 judges and Osiris, who was in charge. They had to convince the judges that they led good lives.

Osiris, *left*, ruled over the afterlife. He would greet people as they entered the afterlife.

People's souls faced Osiris in the Hall of Judgement for the Weighing of the Heart ceremony.

Next, dead souls had to face the Weighing of the Heart ceremony. The Egyptians believed hearts had records of people's actions during their lives. Hearts were weighed on a scale with a feather that represented truth and justice. If a heart was heavier than the feather, the person would be gone forever. But if the scales were balanced, he or she could meet Osiris in the afterlife. Osiris controlled all the vegetation in the afterlife. He made it a place with many flowers, crops, and other plants. It was always springtime in the afterlife.

Explore Online

Watch the video on the website below. Does it give any new evidence to support Chapter Two?

The Weighing of the Heart

abdocorelibrary.com/osiris

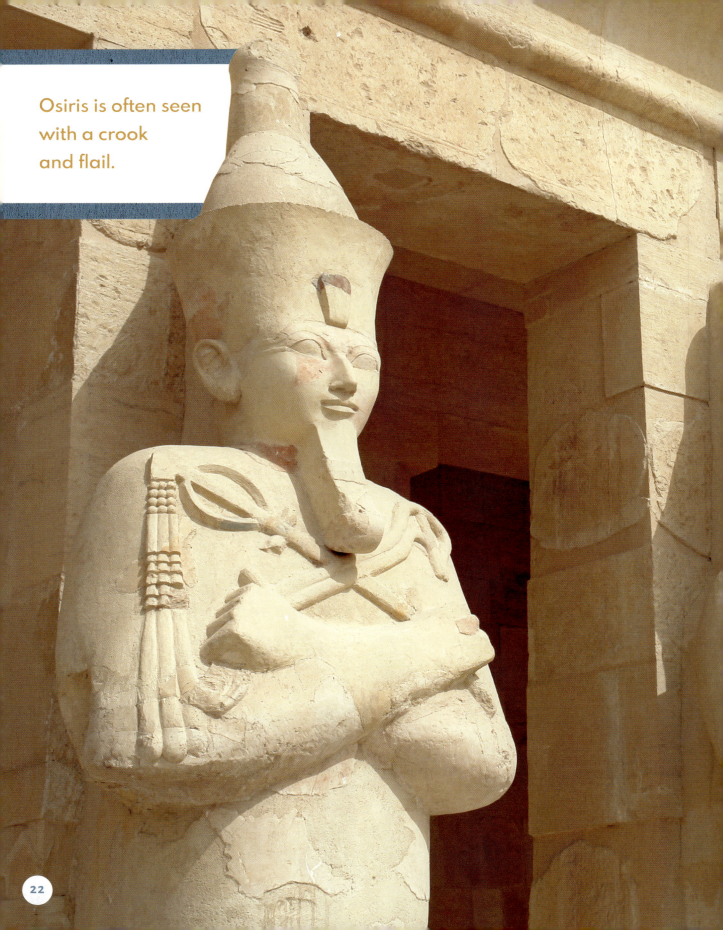

Osiris is often seen with a crook and flail.

CHAPTER 3

OSIRIS IN ART

The ancient Egyptians created many paintings and statues of Osiris. Egyptian art included many symbols. Some of these represent Osiris's royalty. He usually held a shepherd's crook and a flail. The crook is a pole with one end shaped like a hook.

When Osiris is shown with green skin, it represents Earth's vegetation.

The flail is a farming tool, decorated with beads and three leather strips. These two items represented kingship. Osiris's tall crown was decorated with ostrich feathers or with a cobra ready to attack enemies.

Osiris's long, braided beard showed that he was a god. His green skin represented plants and rebirth. He was wrapped as a mummy to show his connection to people who have died.

God of the Dead

Osiris was one of the first gods included in the funeral texts of the Egyptians. These texts included prayers and spells for Osiris's blessing. For example, the *Book of the Dead* contained hymns, or holy songs. Many of these hymns were written to Osiris.

Field of Reeds

The Egyptian afterlife was known as the Field of Reeds. It was just like Egypt, only perfect. There were rivers, fields, and blue skies. Each person was given a plot of land to grow crops. Small statues called shabtis helped them with their work.

This statuette of Osiris shows him in his typical mummy form.

The Egyptians wanted to be reborn like Osiris was. They wanted to meet him in the afterlife. They used him as a model for the first mummy. When someone important died, his or her body was mummified, just like Osiris. This process preserved the body. That way, the soul would be able to live in the body in the afterlife.

The story of Osiris was important to the ancient Egyptians. When he was alive, he helped them establish their civilization. After he died, he judged them in the Hall of Judgement. Osiris represented hope for a happy afterlife.

Further Evidence

Look at the website below. Does it give any new evidence to support Chapter Three?

Statuette of Osiris

abdocorelibrary.com/osiris

LEGENDARY FACTS

Osiris was a god and the first king of Egypt.

Osiris ruled as a good and powerful king until his brother Seth killed him.

When Osiris was brought back to life by Isis, he became the god of the afterlife.

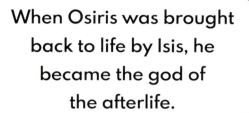

If a person's soul made it through the judgement, he or she met Osiris in the afterlife.

Glossary

afterlife
in ancient Egypt, a place where a person's spirit goes after death

fastened
to have closed firmly or locked

fertility
the ability to produce farm crops or other plant life

jackal
an animal closely related to wolves and dogs that eats weak or dead animals

marshes
areas of muddy, wet land

mummification
the process of preserving a body after death

orally
something that is spoken instead of written

symbolized
represented a certain quality or idea using an object

Online Resources

To learn more about Osiris, visit our free resource websites below.

Visit **abdocorelibrary.com** or scan this QR code for free Common Core resources for teachers and students, including vetted activities, multimedia, and booklinks, for deeper subject comprehension.

Visit **abdobooklinks.com** or scan this QR code for free additional online weblinks for further learning. These links are routinely monitored and updated to provide the most current information available.

Learn More

Alexander, Heather. *A Child's Introduction to Egyptology.* Black Dog & Leventhal, 2021.

Honovich, Nancy. *1,000 Facts about Ancient Egypt.* National Geographic, 2019.

Index

afterlife, 8, 17–21, 25, 26–27
Anubis, 8, 17

Byblos, 7, 9

coffin, 7, 9, 13
crook, 23–24

fertility, 16, 17
Field of Reeds, 18, 25
flail, 23–24

hieroglyphs, 12
hymns, 25

Isis, 5, 7–8, 17

jackal, 17

mummification, 8, 25–27

Nephthys, 8
Nile River, 7–9, 17

Seth, 5–8, 13, 15–17

Weighing of the Heart ceremony, 20–21

About the Author

Samantha S. Bell lives in the foothills of the Blue Ridge Mountains. She has written more than 100 nonfiction books for kids on topics ranging from penguins to tractors to surviving on a deserted island.